Christian Clip Art

Volume 3

Author:
Sherrill B. Flora

Artists:
"Our Best!"

Cover Art:
Kristina VanOss

Cover Production:
Annette Hollister-Papp

Contents

Angels 2-3	Ea...
Bibles 4-5	Jesus...
Borders 6-8	Names of...
Children/Families ... 9-13	Noah's Ark ......
Christmas 14-20	Plants of the Bible 39-40
Contemporary Christian Symbols 21-23	Prayer 41-42
Crosses 224-25	Scripture 43-45
Doves 26	Stained Glass 46-47
	Words 48

Copyright Notice

In Celebration™ grants the right to the individual purchaser to reproduce the materials in this book for noncommercial individual, classroom or church use only. Reproduction for an entire school or school system is strictly prohibited. No part of this publication may be reproduced for storage in a retrieval system, or transmitted in any form or by any means, electronic, mechanical, recording, or otherwise, without the prior written permission of the publisher. For information regarding permission write to: In Celebration™, P.O. Box 1650, Grand Rapids, MI 49501.

Standard Book Number: 1-56822-539-3
UPC: 0 13587 23794 6
SPCN: 990-219-3331
Christian Clip Art, Vol. 3
© 1997 by In Celebration™
A division of Instructional Fair • TS Denison
2400 Turner Avenue NW
Grand Rapids, Michigan 49544

Angels

In Celebration™   2   IF9503 Christian Clip Art

Angels

In Celebration™ 3 IF9503 Christian Clip Art

Bibles

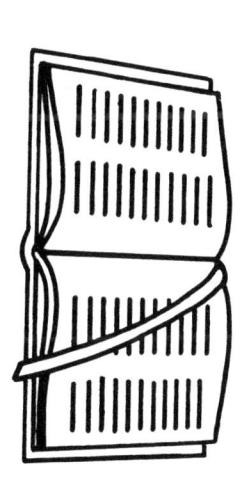

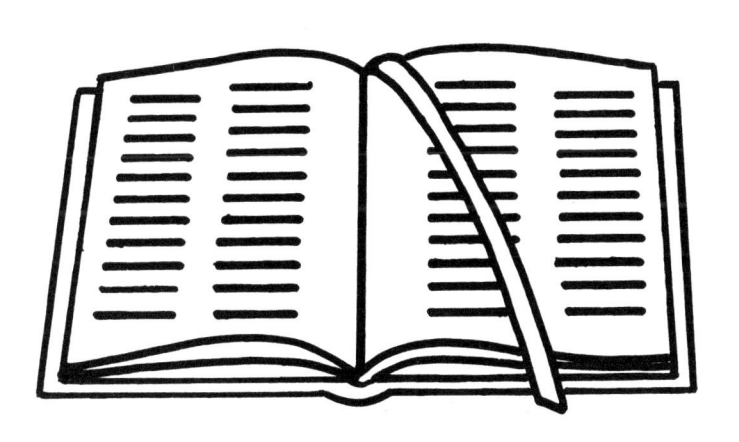

In Celebration™   IF9503 Christian Clip Art

Bibles

HOLY BIBLE

In Celebration™   5   IF9503 Christian Clip Art

Borders

Praise The Lord!

God made me special

Praise The Lord!

In the Name of the Father, of the Son, and of the Holy Spirit.

In Celebration™ — IF9503 Christian Clip Art

Borders

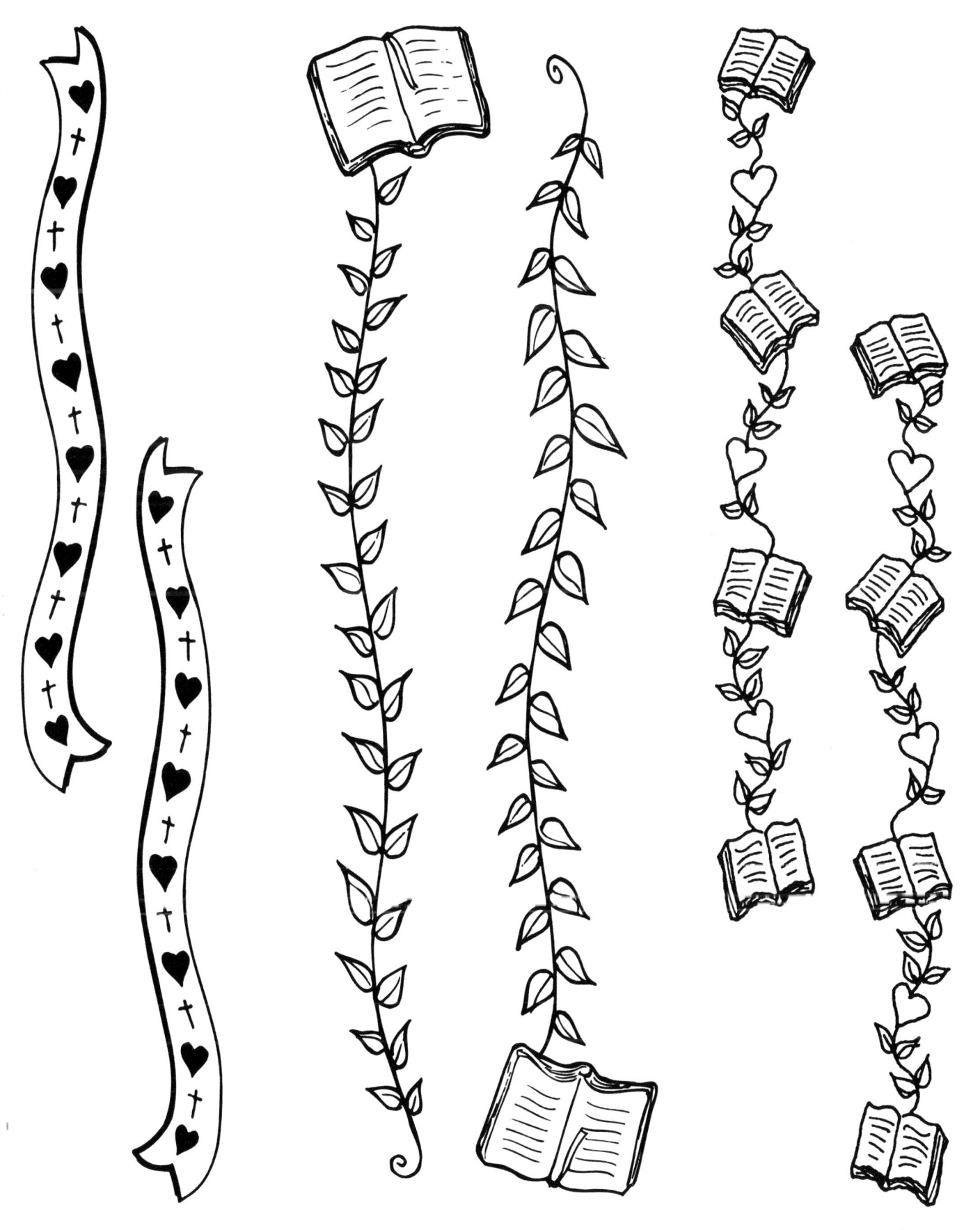

In Celebration™ 7 IF9503 Christian Clip Art

Borders

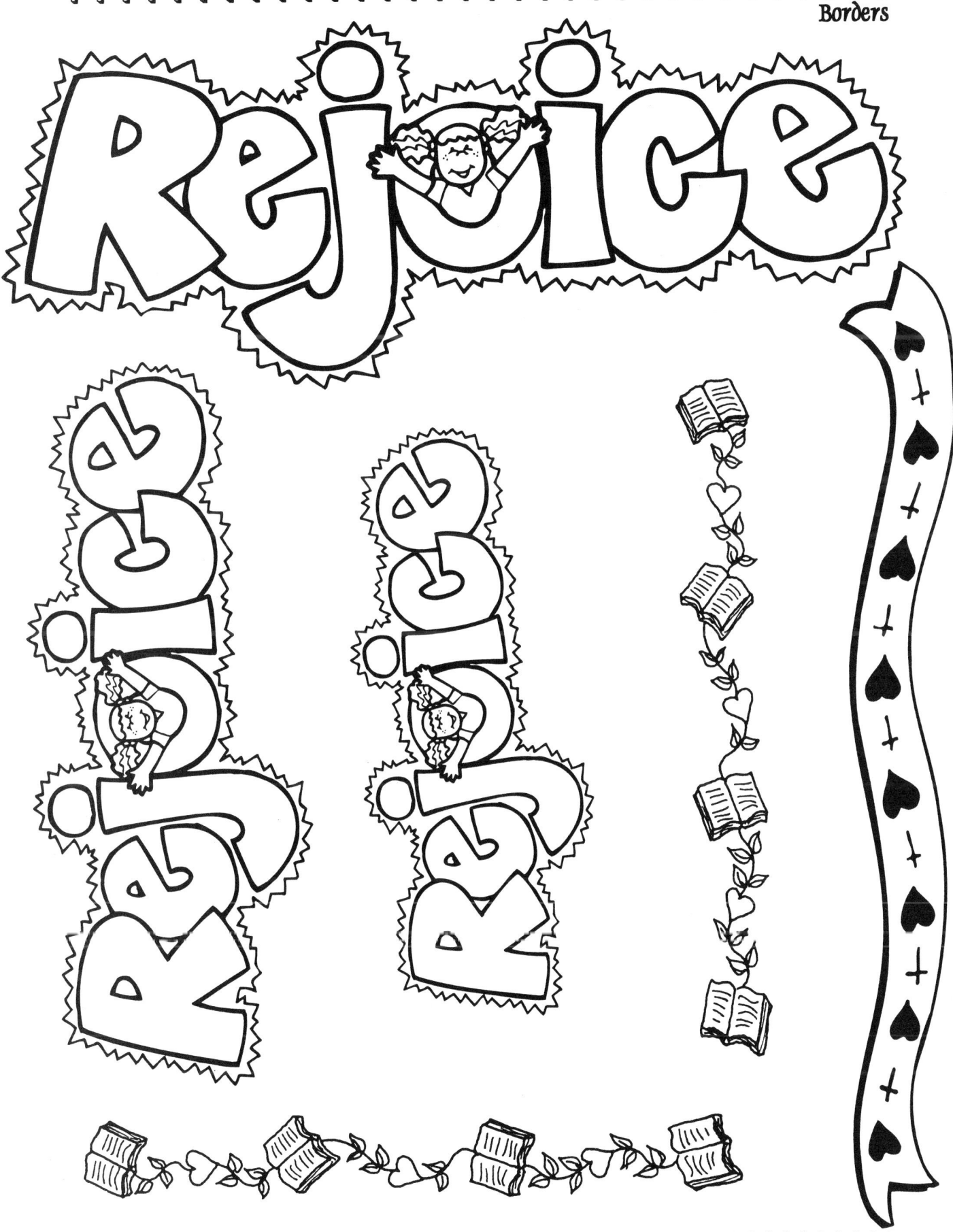

Rejoice

Rejoice Rejoice

In Celebration™ · 8 · IF9503 Christian Clip Art

Children & Families

In Celebration™ 9 IF9503 Christian Clip Art

Children & Families

In Celebration   10   IF9503 Christian Clip Art

Children & Families

In Celebration — II — IF9503 Christian Clip Art

Children & Families

In Celebration™ — 12 — IF9503 Christian Clip Art

Children & Families

In Celebration™ · IF9503 Christian Clip Art

Christmas

In Celebration™   14   IF9503 Christian Clip Art

Christmas

In Celebration   15   IF9503 Christian Clip Art

Christmas

In Celebration™   17   IF9503 Christian Clip Art

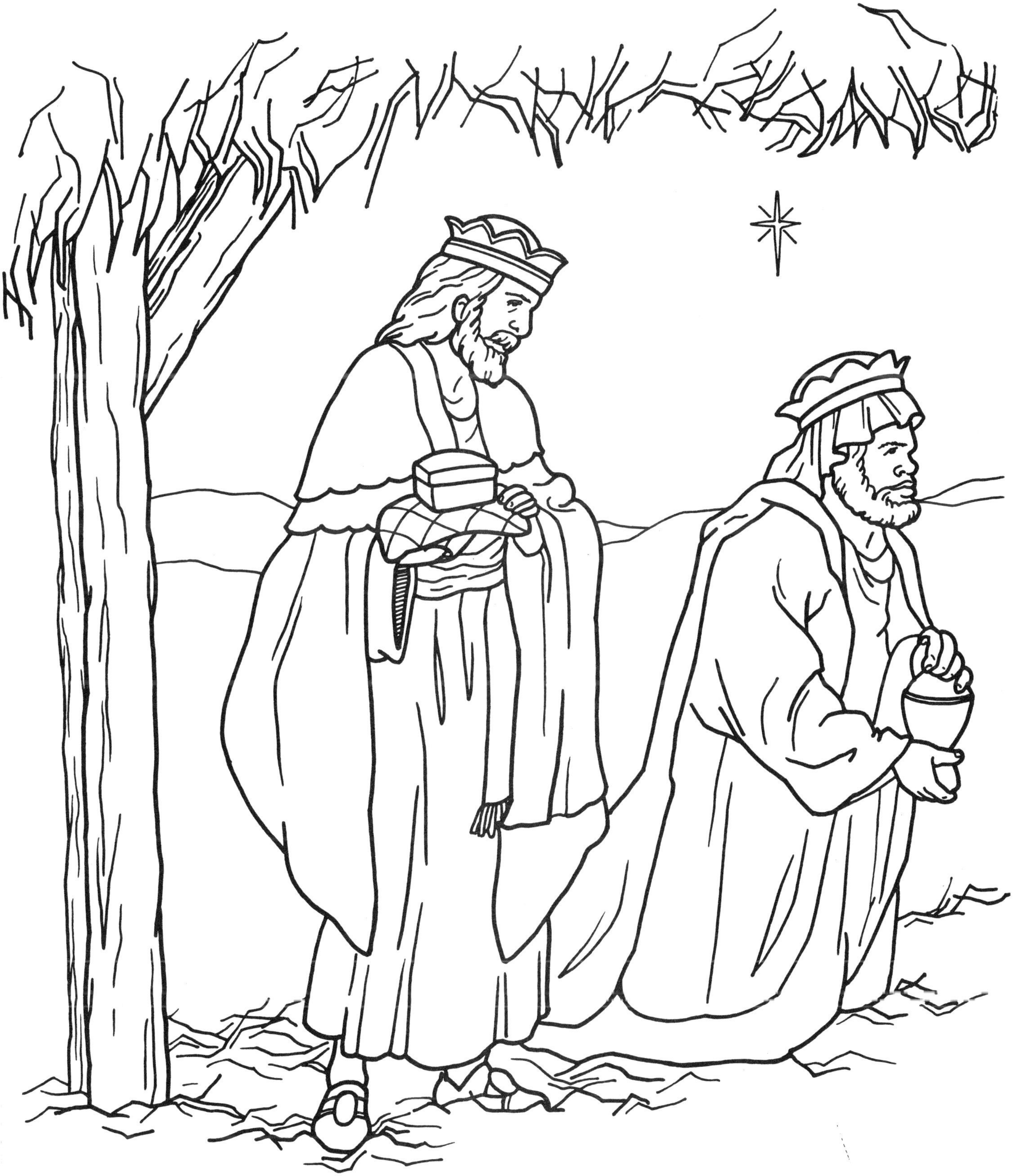

In Celebration™   19   IF9503 Christian Clip Art

Christmas

Contemporary Christian Symbols

In Celebration™ 21 IF9503 Christian Clip Art

Contemporary Christian Symbols

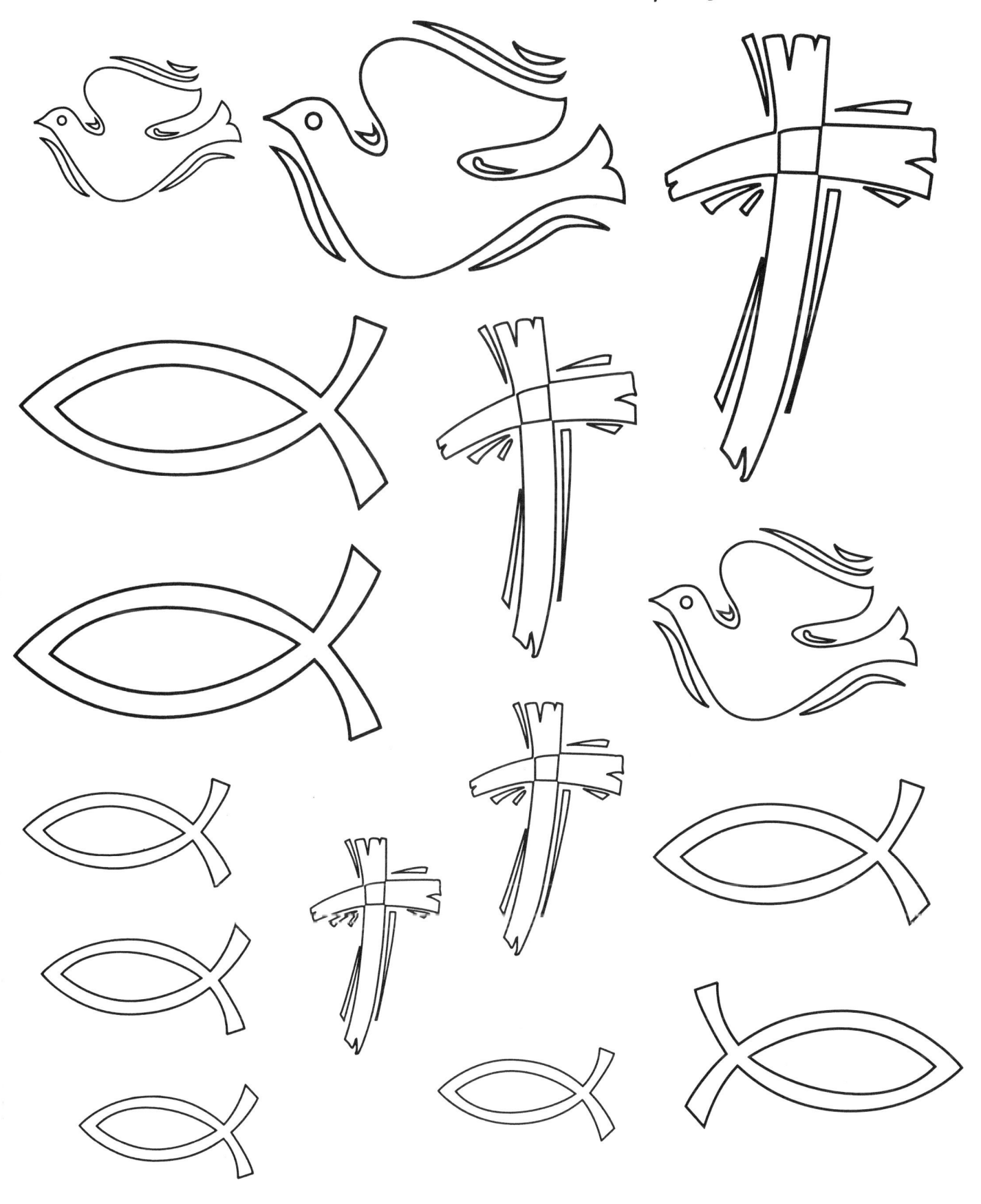

In Celebration™   22   IF9503 Christian Clip Art

Contemporary Christian Symbols

In Celebration™ — IF9503 Christian Clip Art

Crosses

In Celebration™ — IF9503 Christian Clip Art

Crosses

In Celebration™ 25 IF9503 Christian Clip Art

Doves

In Celebration™ 26 IF9503 Christian Clip Art

Easter

In Celebration™   27   IF9503 Christian Clip Art

Easter

In Celebration™ 28 IF9503 Christian Clip Art

Easter

In Celebration™ 29 IF9503 Christian Clip Art

Jesus & the Children

In Celebration™ — 30 — IF9503 Christian Clip Art

Jesus & the Children

In Celebration
31
IF9503 Christian Clip Art

Jesus & the Children

In Celebration   32   IF9503 Christian Clip Art

Names of God

Prince of Peace

King of Kings

The Good Shepherd

The Light of the World

Mighty God

Messiah

Mighty God

Jesus

Emmanuel

Everlasting Father

Noah's Ark

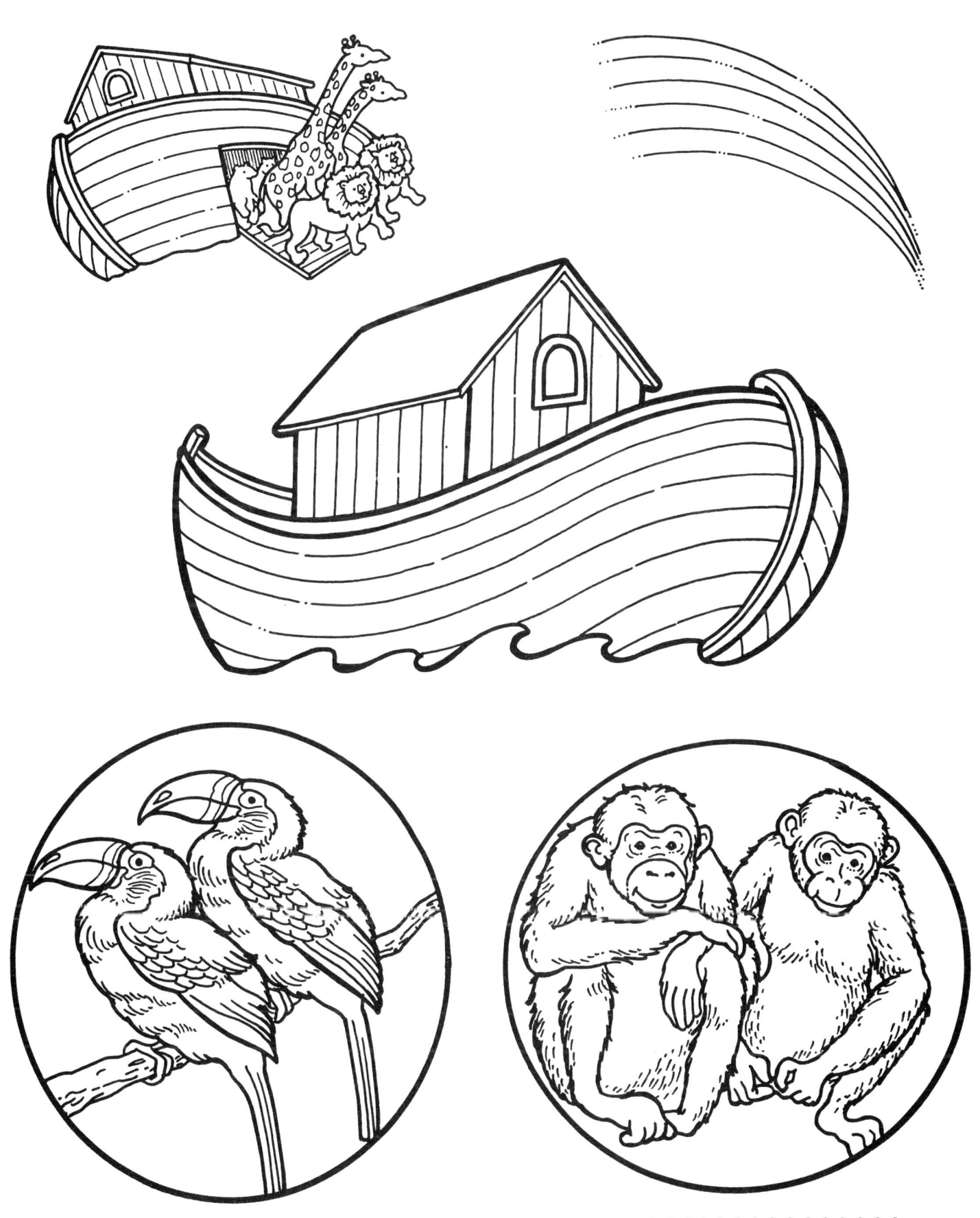

In Celebration™ 34 IF9503 Christian Clip Art

Noah's Ark

In Celebration™   35   IF9503 Christian Clip Art

Noah's Ark

In Celebration™ 36 IF9503 Christian Clip Art

Noah's Ark

Noah's Ark

In Celebration™   38   IF9503 *Christian Clip Art*

Plants of the Bible

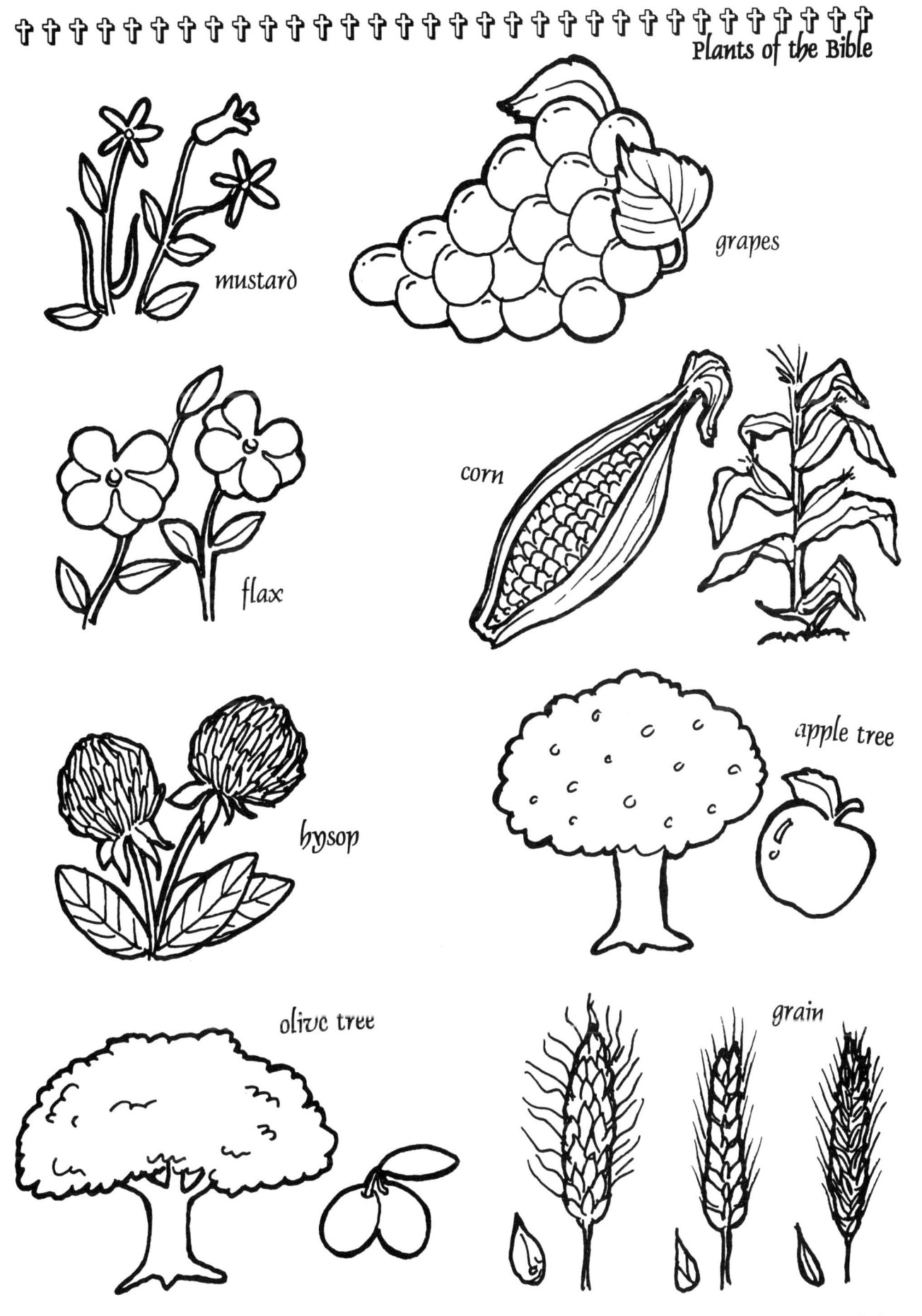

mustard

grapes

flax

corn

hysop

apple tree

olive tree

grain

Plants of the Bible

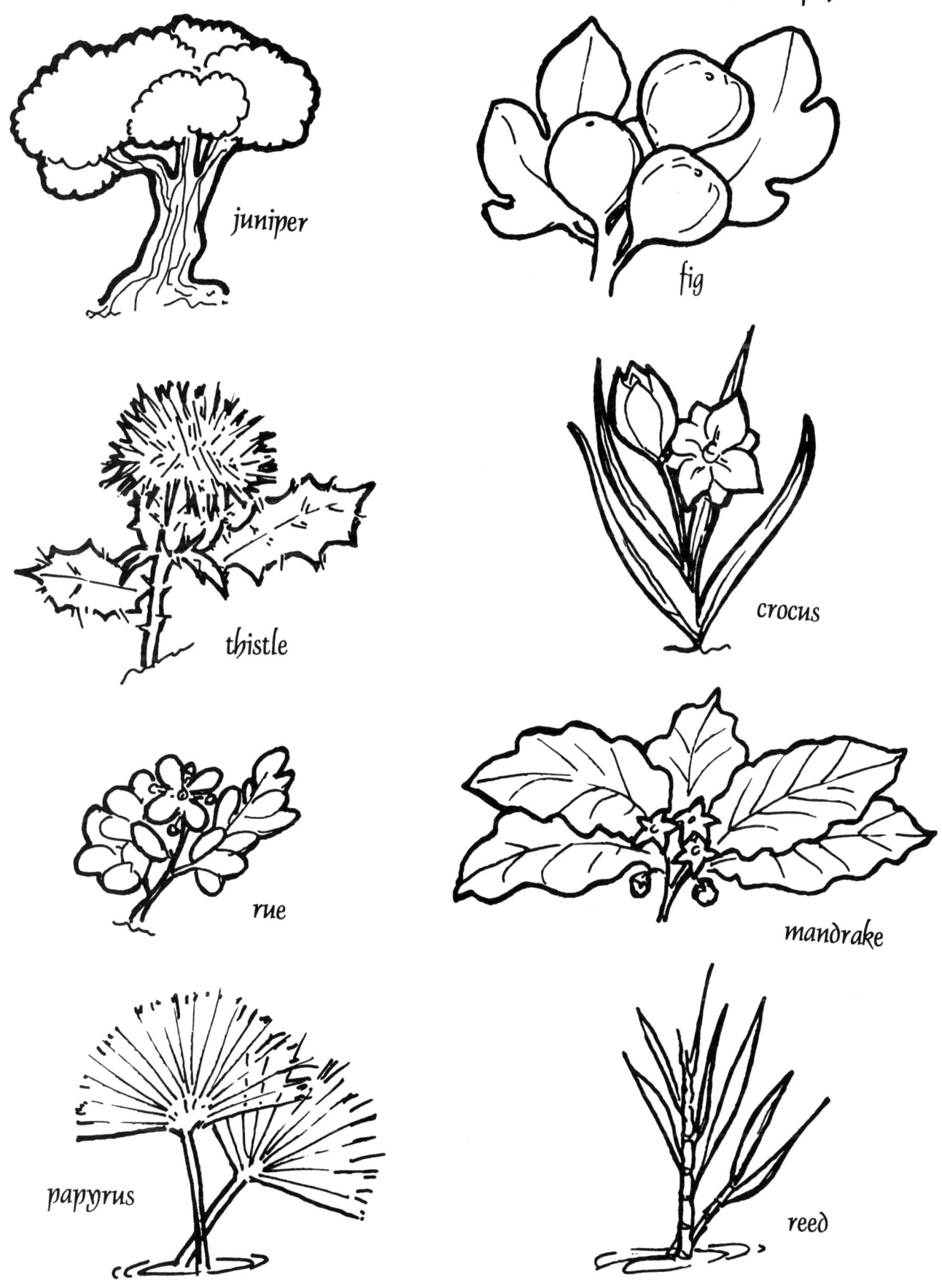

juniper

fig

thistle

crocus

rue

mandrake

papyrus

reed

Prayer/Praying Hands

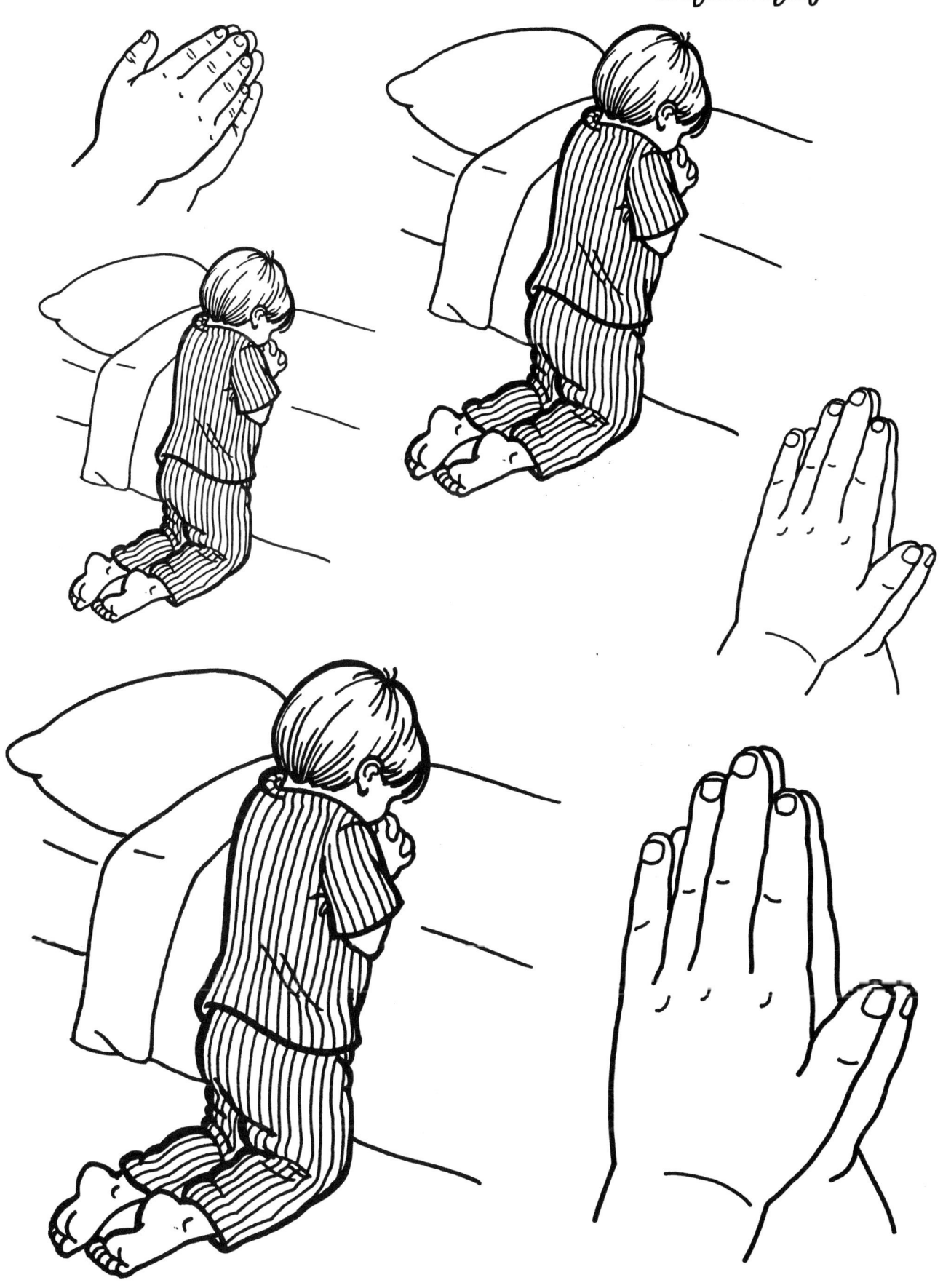

41

In Celebration — IF9503 Christian Clip Art

Prayer/Praying Hands

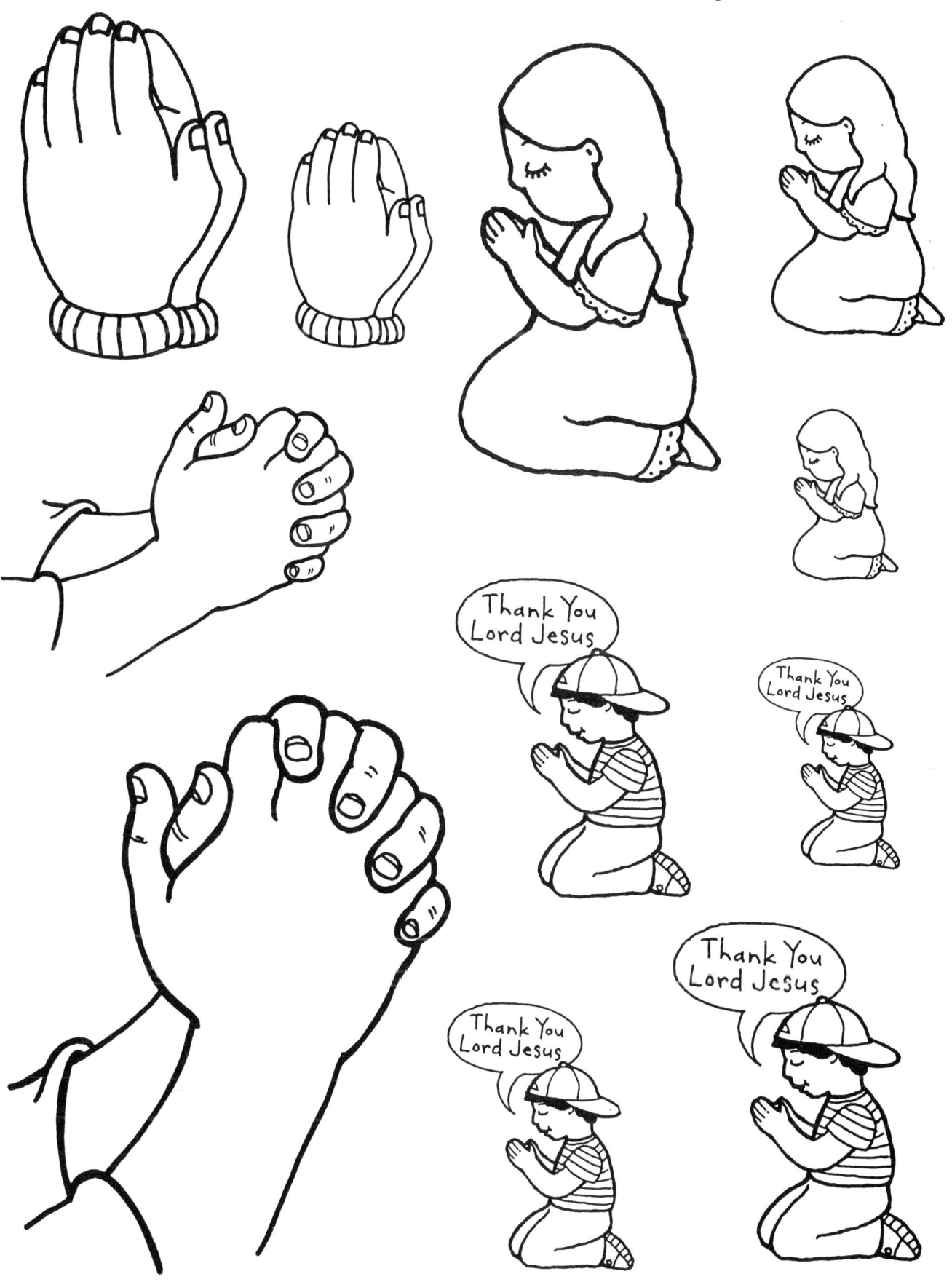

In Celebration   42   IF9503 Christian Clip Art

Scripture

"Your Word is a lamp to my feet and a light for my path."
Psalm 119:105

"Your Word is a lamp to my feet and a light for my path."
Psalm 119:105

"For nothing is impossible with God."
Luke 1:37

"Your Word is a lamp to my feet and a light for my path."
Psalm 119:105

"For nothing is impossible with God."
Luke 1:37

"For nothing is impossible with God."
Luke 1:37

"FOR NOTHING IS IMPOSSIBLE WITH GOD."
LUKE 1:37

"For nothing is impossible with God."
Luke 1:37

"IN THE BEGINNING WAS THE WORD, AND THE WORD WAS WITH GOD, AND THE WORD WAS GOD."
JOHN 1:1

"HE ALONE IS MY ROCK AND MY SALVATION; HE IS MY FORTRESS, I WILL NOT BE SHAKEN."

PSALM 62:6

"He alone is my rock and my salvation; he is my fortress, I will not be shaken."

Psalm 62:6

"He alone is my rock and my salvation; he is my fortress, I will not be shaken."

Psalm 62:6

"For God so loved the world that he gave his one and only Son, and whoever believes in him shall not perish but have eternal life."

John 3:16

"For God so loved the world that he gave his one and only Son, and whoever believes in him shall not perish but have eternal life."

John 3:16

"For God so loved the world that he gave his one and only Son, and whoever believes in him shall not perish but have eternal life."

John 3:16

Scripture

"Rejoice in the Lord always."
Philippians 4:4

"Rejoice in the Lord always."
Philippians 4:4

"Rejoice
in the Lord always."
Philippians 4:4

"REJOICE
IN THE LORD ALWAYS."
PHILIPPIANS 4:4

"For it is by grace you have been saved,
through faith . . it is the gift of God."
Ephesians 2:8

"For it is by grace you have been saved,
through faith . .
it is the gift of God."
Ephesians 2:8

"For it is by grace
you have been saved,
through faith . .
it is the gift of God."
Ephesians 2:8

'For it is by grace you have been saved,
through faith . . ,
it is the gift of God.'

Ephesians 2:8

Stained Glass

In Celebration™ — 46 — IF9503 Christian Clip Art

Stained Glass

Rejoice in the Lord

In Celebration
47
IF9503 Christian Clip Art

Words

love

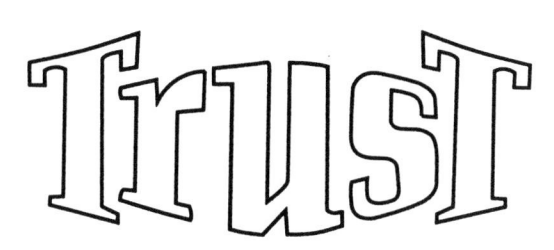

trust

Awesome God

grace

Awesome God

Praise

My God is an Awesome God

joy

Awesome God

faith

In Celebration
48
IF9503 Christian Clip Art